I0162988

Be Not Ignorant Brethren

Richard Mallette, TH.D.

Empyrion Publishing
Winter Garden FL
info@EmpyrionPublishing.com

Be Not Ignorant Brethren

Richard Mallette, TH.D.

Be Not Ignorant Brethren
ISBN: 978-0692213674
Copyright 2014 by Richard Mallette, TH.D.

Empyrion Publishing
Winter Garden FL
info@EmpyrionPublishing.com

Unless otherwise indicated, all Scripture quotations are taken from the King James Version of the bible.

I have deliberately chosen to place the name 'satan' in the lower case letters, because he deserves no courtesy.

Printed in the United States of America. All rights reserved under international copyright laws. Contents and/or cover may not be reproduced in whole or in part in any form without the express written consent of the author.

Acknowledgement and Dedication

With sincere thanks to Paloma Mallette, my daughter-in-law for her hard work in transferring my notes into a readable transcript.

I dedicate this book to my family:

Lauren
Richard, Jr.
Juliana
Nathaniel

And my dear wife, Adrienne, who always encourages me in all things

Table of Contents

Author's Preface

The purpose of this book is to point out that there are many ignorances within our human race. We refer to some people who have these ignorances, at times, as being dysfunctional. We will try to define dysfunctional and of course, who are those who are functional?

We will focus on Christianity as having her share of dysfunctional Believers, though we will call them ignorant Christians.

Among our Christian brothers and sisters, there are those that are lazy, indifferent, and some who very clearly refuse to believe the Word of God. Many of these Christians find themselves just repeating what others in their circle say, and have no regard for what the Word really says. Some just are happy living in their Biblical ignorance.

I am not setting myself above anybody just because I've chosen to write this book. I, too, had labored in some of the same ignorances I write about.

For years, I just represented what those Christians with whom I associated, and thought that what I believed was accurate Biblically, too.

After 30 years of pastoring, and upon my temporary retirement, I found the time to study for myself instead of a weekly preparation for others.

Over time, as I found out, and with careful study, and meditation, I began to see the errors in my thinking concerning God's Word.

I questioned my closely held beliefs. I kept on asking God if I had the full truth on many subjects.

Eventually, I was able to take the truths I had, alter them, change certain ways of explaining them, and adding new depth to them. I even dropped some things I thought were the truth.

During this time I discovered why people, sincere Christians, made these mistakes as I did, and have found how to receive God's truth, and be comfortable with the results. My faith in God grew. My confidence in my ability to hear God's thoughts grew, and my confidence in my ability to hear God's Spirit increased, and what I have learned hopefully can profit others.

In Chapter 5, I will give you ways to avoid being taken in by being ignorant of God's Word.

I will show you how to dig out the real nuggets of truth, and the truth will make you free.

Read this book with an open mind, check the things I will say against God's Word to verify what was said. This is your challenge and opportunity to grow.

As you read through the New Testament, you will come across one particular statement warning Christians not to be caught up in ignorance. Out of these ten times it is written under various occasions and circumstances, one in particular caught my eye.

In 1 Peter 2:15 Peter says:

"For so is the Will of God, that with well doing you may put to silence the ignorance of foolish men."

I'm willing to take that duty, and consider it a privilege from God to, at least, clean up some misconceptions, and even outright untruths.

CHAPTER

1

Dysfunctional Christians

There is a lot of talk today about dysfunctional families and individuals. The so-called experts on this subject have their own definition of dysfunctional. I suppose to arrive at a definition of dysfunctional they would have to know what is functional.

A functional family, I have heard them say, is a group of individuals bound together with a father and/or mother or with both and one or more children. And there should be seen some kind of development and some sort of maintenance of certain performances that are accepted by a society, and can perform within certain preset norms within that society.

I am no psychologist, but a teacher of God's

Word, a pastor who has been given the position to oversee both individuals and families, and I can agree with some definition of dysfunction to a degree, because they usually leave God out of their discussions of what their definition is. Dysfunction usually occurs when God is just someone we go to when we are in a jam. He is very functional, and knows how we should function.

So let's look at what dysfunctional must be. They, the experts that I have heard over the years, have said that a dysfunctional individual is one who has abnormal or impaired ability to function to a standard set by society. Of course, that same rule applies to a family.

So, our society has set a norm of what they call functional or dysfunctional, and for the most part, we can agree that there are both functional and dysfunctional families and individuals.

But have you ever considered that within the family of God, with both individuals and family units, that there could be those who would be called dysfunctional? I'm speaking about Christians, believers in Jesus Christ.

Listen, when one is saved, it is his spirit that receives the Life of Christ, and the soul, which contains the intellect (that is, the mind) and the emotions and the will, are not changed.

The Word of God tells us to renew our

14

minds. We do that through the reading, study and meditation of God's Word. Then we act on the Word. We live according to God's Word.

It is not impossible for a dysfunctional person to hold down a job and function fairly well at it. There are millions of these dysfunctional persons all around us just about everywhere.

And there are times that the "more normal" people around them recognize that something is missing in these people. It is not that they are without common sense regarding most things, they are not stupid people, and we allow them to function around us without much concern, for the most part. These people are abnormally, normal.

Now don't you think that it is possible that our churches have their fair share of these dysfunctional individuals and families? These dysfunctional individuals and families in our churches are the ones who feel that they have a need for counseling by their pastor, and some don't recognize they need help in any area of their lives.

Yes, some know they need help. But the thing that is so disturbing to me, as a pastor, is that they can verbalize what they think their problem is, and sometimes they are very accurate, and yet, when they are given the solution to their problem, they cannot even try to do what will get rid of their problem. They won't even try.

I have pondered this and the answer seems

to vary with each individual, but when you dig a little deeper, you'll find they really do not want to change. And, this resistance to the changes you suggest to help them, because in reality, they like where they are at, and the question now becomes, are they lazy or ignorant?

I eliminated lazy, because they do hold down jobs, they go to work every day. So I have concluded that their attitude and their lack of the proper knowledge, and not wanting to improve their circumstances, is nothing more than ignorance.

I'm not looking for some psychologist to write me and say I am wrong, but, and before you do, listen to what these people tell me, more than not, even after I tell them God's Word is simple, and even a child can understand it. They say, "I don't think I can do that." "But why?" I ask them. Then the verification of this ignorance comes flying at you because the truth is now spoken while they answer your "why can't you do what God suggests?"

"Well," they say, "I've been taught all my life that it's this way because we've always done it this way." It doesn't even matter what God's word says, to the people. It's almost like tradition. They are stuck in their ways.

Somewhere down the line someone told them such and such, so, in the case of a church person, they will tell you how spiritual that person was who told them, "...so, I am sure of what you are telling me, is your interpretation."

"No, I just read it word for word out of the bible."

Then they say, "I can't accept that, no offense intended" They resist the truth of God's Word, and cling to what they have heard for years and continue to repeat it with no true understanding that it is not Bible truth.

That my dear readers, is absolute ignorance.

No wonder Paul and Peter kept saying to the church, "I would not have you to be ignorant, brethren."

So let's look at what Christians say that is born out of ignorance, pure ignorance of God's Word. What's so dangerous, is, what they keep repeating is passed to generation after generation. And this untruth, this ignorance is passed on.

I call it moral ignorance in many cases, because it defies Biblical understanding because they refuse to study the Word. They just insist they are right. Nevertheless, it is some kind of ignorance. You have heard this as I have so many times.

When a Christian can't explain why certain things that have happened, especially a tragic thing, like a child dying of a dreadful disease or a murder, they will answer you with, "Well, you know God is sovereign."

If you ask them what that means, they say, "God is God, so He can do anything, you know, He's sovereign." That is ignorance of God's Word.

Yes, of course, God is sovereign, and very few will deny that fact. But not everyone knows that God's sovereignty is limited to His Word, when He is dealing with people, His dealings are confined to His Word, or He cannot hold us responsible for our actions. We are held responsible to comply with His Word. He is Just with us.

He cannot pull an ace out of the hat, something that is not in His Word, and hold us responsible. You can certainly understand this?

His sovereignty is always within His Word, and therefore He can hold us responsible, if we have heard the Word, and just disobey it.

And when they say He is sovereign in the context I gave, they are implying that God caused the tragedy and killed that child or caused the disease. That is pure ignorance of God's Word. God is the giver of life. Didn't Jesus come that you might have a more abundant life? And what about this scripture?

Isaiah 54:14-15

"In righteousness shalt thou be established: thou shalt be far from oppression; for thou shalt not fear: and from

terror; for it shall not come near thee. Behold, they shall surely gather together, but not by me: whoever shall gather together against thee shall fall for thysake."

James 1:13

"Let no man say when he is tempted, I am tempted of God: for God cannot be tempted with evil, neither tempteth He anyman."

We are talking about the Christian, the one who is morally ignorant. This Christian thinks that because God is sovereign that He can do what He pleases, even kill children, and He is the one who has something to do with murder, or terrorists, or mental atrocities.

What else could they mean when a tragedy takes place and they can't explain it? They again, say, "You know God is sovereign."

I have never gotten an explanation from any of them of what they mean. I guess they heard someone say that and they picked it up and ran with it. It became part of their Biblical vocabulary.

Here's another statement that Christians say so often, and it shows their ignorance of God's Word.

Oh, yes, they quote scripture all the time, and they contradict so much of the Word that it is sad. Their study of the Word is superficial. These are the people who also read what they believe in the bible. But they don't believe what they read. They say, "God is so mysterious, you'll never know what He will do."

Really? In which way is God mysterious? If they answer you, listen to them struggle with it.

God is not mysterious. And perhaps He may still be holding back some mysteries that He may reveal, someday. But now, the Bible and the Holy Spirit is your guide. And yes, God does have secrets. Look at Deuteronomy 29:29.

"The secret things belong unto the Lord our God: but those things which are revealed belong unto us and to our children forever, that we may do all the words of this law."

God does have secrets. God knows when you and I will die. He has a lot of secrets, but it says nothing about His being mysterious anywhere, in His dealings with us. We can't pull that out of context to make it fit our beliefs. All mysteries, if you refer to them as mysteries when you don't know enough about the Bible to explain it. The Bible is easily understood with adequate study.

God has held mysteries for generations and ages, but has revealed them, such as what Paul has spoken about in his Epistles, those things about

Jesus taking our sins into His spirit and dying for us. Paul reveals the mystery of our redemption, hid for ages.

The Bible is God's Will, written so we can know what God's purpose is for our lives. His Word is a blueprint for us to follow, and it will lead us into paths that will please God.

Where is the mystery? There is no mystery about God...He is not mysterious. We can know what He will do, His Word declares Him in all His majesty. His ways have been shown to us.

Again, these things that Christians say are because they are ignorant of what God's Word says. They need to dig deeper and ask the Holy Spirit to open up the Word and give them Revelation-Knowledge.

So, as I go from Chapter to Chapter, I will tell you the truths that Christians don't know.

They are, in reality, speaking the opposite of what God says. They contradict God. They even call Him a Liar without realizing it. God can still accept them on the basis of the Moral Light they have.

For example, I have heard someone say that they thank God for their pain. That contradicts so many scriptures. It actually is calling God a Liar. Again, this arises out of ignorance.

Or you may hear, "I am suffering for God's glory." Do you know when enough suffering will glorify God? There are so many ignorances being repeated daily.

Here's the top of the list. "It's God's Will that I am sick." Well, then, if it is God's Will, why do you take medicine and go to the doctor, that would be *not* keeping His Will, wouldn't it?

So let's us try to bring some sense to these senseless, unbiblical statements and understand the truth. That would give God glory, and that truth will make you free.

CHAPTER

2

Sense-Knowledge vs.

Revelation-Knowledge

First of all let me show you some examples of what I will call Sense-Knowledge Faith.

Acts 2:1-4

"And when the day of Pentecost was fully come, they were all with one accord in one place. And suddenly there came a sound from heaven as of a rushing mighty wind, and it filled all the house where they were sitting. And there appeared unto them cloven tongues like as of

fire, and it sat upon each of them. And they were all filled with the Holy Ghost, and began to speak with other tongues, as the Spirit gave them utterance."

Let's look at this:

- they heard the sound of the rushing of a mighty wind
- they saw the tongues like as of fire parting asunder upon each one
- they heard them speak in tongues

So the faith they had at that moment was purely Sense-Knowledge Faith. They believed in tongues because they heard them speak in tongues. In 1 John 1:1-4 it brings out Sense-Knowledge even more clearly. It says:

"That which was from the beginning, which we have heard, which we have seen with our eyes, which we have looked upon, and our hands have handled, of the Word of life; (For the life was manifested, and we have seen *it*, and bear witness, and shew unto you that eternal life, which was with the Father, and was manifested unto us;) That which we have seen and heard, declare we unto you..."

Again, their faith was based on what their senses told them.

It is a fact that from our birth, all of our education comes through five channels, sight, hearing, smelling, tasting and touching.

This is called knowledge we have accumulated through our five senses. We call this kind of knowledge Sense-Knowledge, and all the knowledge that man put together over the centuries, comes from their senses.

That realm of the senses that scientists live in, produces all they know and can expound on. Eventually, when they can go no further, they then invent theories, and much is guess work.

They cannot admit that there are limits to Sense-Knowledge, and either they do not know there is another realm where knowledge can come from, or they won't acknowledge it.

If Darwin knew of this other realm, and could have gotten into it, he never would have written the book that damned millions of people with his Evolutionary Theory.

What is that other realm I am talking about? Peter in his confrontation with Jesus first heard about it from Jesus.

In Matthew 16:13 - Jesus asked His disciples, **"Whom do men say that I, the Son of Man am?"**

Their answers included men like John the

Baptist, Elijah, Jeremiah and or one of the prophets.

Jesus said to them, **"But whom say ye that I am?** Peter answered and said, **"Thou are the Christ, the Son of the Living God."**

And Jesus said unto him, **"Blessed are thou, Simon Barjona: for flesh and blood hath not revealed** *it* **unto thee, but my Father which is in heaven."**

When Jesus said that Peter didn't get this from flesh and blood, He meant it didn't come out of your natural knowledge you get from your senses, but God, Himself, revealed this to you.

Jesus introduced, very clearly, that all knowledge doesn't come from our senses. There is another realm called the spiritual realm, and out of this realm comes Revelation-Knowledge. We call this revealed knowledge.

1 Corinthians 2:9-14 explains this very clearly to the unbiased listener.

"But as it is written, Eye hath not seen, nor ear heard, neither have entered into the heart of man, the things which God hath prepared for them that love Him."

(So far He has said that the senses play no part in this, neither the heart.) **"But God hath** revealed them unto us by His spirit, for the spirit searcheth all things, yea the deep things of God. For what man knoweth the things of a man, save the spirit of man which is in him? Even though the things of God knoweth no man; but the Spirit of God. Now we have received not the spirit of the world, but the Spirit which is of God, that we might know the things that are freely given to us of God. Which things also we speak, not in the words which man's wisdom teacheth, (or things out of his five senses) but which the Holy Ghost teacheth, comparing spiritual things with spiritual." (In other words, spiritual things have nothing to do with what the senses can know.)

"But the natural man receiveth not the things of the Spirit of God, for they are foolish unto him, neither can he know them because they are spiritually discerned."

Above when He refers to the natural man, the word natural in the Greek language is the word PSUCHIKOS (pronounced as *psoo-khee-kos.*) It means of the sensual, or of the sense. You cannot spiritually discern anything as we have just read, without the Holy Spirit.

His job is to lead or guide you to all truth. He won't speak of Himself, but **"...Whatsoever He**

shall hear, [that] shall He speak: and He will shew you things to come." (John 16:13)

Sense-knowledge Christians have refused to believe much about what the Bible says about the Holy Spirit.

Paul, the Apostle, was given revelation concerning the Holy Spirit and what was revealed to Paul, so that the Believer could know the spiritual truths of the Word, as Paul said, **"...the things that are freely given to us..."**

These Christians become ignorant because they refuse to accept the revelation that the Spirit gave us that pertains to life and Godliness.

Because of Sense-Knowledge that prevails among most Christians, their lives will never reach what Jesus paid for through His great substitutionary work of Redemption.

Their Sense-Knowledge teachings keep them, not only from receiving what Jesus paid for, they often call God a Liar. Most will deny this, but nevertheless, it is the truth.

Here's an example. They thank God for any pain they have, and through ignorance of His Word, they say at the same time, "I'm standing in faith."

What kind of faith is that? You are saying that God gave you the pain, then pop aspirins for the pain. If God gave it to you, then why do you take something to get rid of the pain? If the pain came from God, as you think, and you thanked Him for it; then skip the aspirin and keep thanking Him.

Then they say, "God won't give me more than I can bear." Well, then if you know that God knows when to take the pain off you once you have taken all you can, just wait until God acknowledges you've reached your limit on pain and He'll pull it off you? Stop running to the doctor, stop all medicine, because in taking medicine you are going against God's will. You must think it is His will for you to have pain, so you are thanking Him for it. So drop the medicine.

Don't be ignorant, brethren. Wake up and read the Bible and believe what you read. Stop believing what your under-informed church or denomination is telling you and start believing the bible. Ask the Holy Spirit to free you daily with God's truth.

By thanking God for your pain, you are calling God a Liar when He said in 1 Peter 2:24 **"...by Whose stripes ye were healed."**

You are contradicting Isaiah 53:4-5 and Matthew 8:16-17. Get out of your ignorance of God's Word. Your lack of Revelation-Knowledge, that is, what God has revealed, has been destroying you. Stop saying what your senses tell you, that is, *"I don't feel good." "I can't see how that will work."*

Listen to me, and don't shut down on me

now. But listen carefully, all things of Romans 8:28 do not always work together for your good, until you follow this scripture in 2 Corinthians 4:17-18, and I will paraphrase it for you.

"For momentary affliction is producing for us an eternal weight of glory far beyond all comparison: while we look not at the things that are seen but at the things that are not seen, for the things that are seen are temporal, but the things that are not seen are eternal."

I am not saying that temptation won't come your way, there will be troubles and sickness, but I am saying that they have no right to continue to be in your life because Jesus, already, as your substitute, carried them for you. Galatians 3:13 tells us we have been redeemed from the curse of the law. The curse was three-fold, eternal death, sickness and poverty. Now back to an explanation of Romans 8:28. Let me explain 2 Corinthians 4:17-18.

The word *"while"* teaches us that affliction serves us only while we keep our eyes on the invisible realm. If we lose sight of it and become preoccupied with the world of time and of the sense we are no longer able to receive the benefits or those things that work for our good.

I had this explanation of 2 Corinthians 4:17-18 concerning Romans 8:28 in the back of my bible, and I think that years ago I got it from something that someone had written, I think. So I'll give them the credit, if that came from another person.

Read the Word. Meditate the Word and your ignorances will soon be replaced with Revelation-Knowledge. Keep your senses out of the way, and you will soon give way to Revelation-Knowledge.

How you felt will not change God's Word. Again, read, study and meditate God's Word, and stop repeating what others have influenced you with misinformation about The Bible, and let God show you the truth through His revelations.

CHAPTER

3

Adam's Sin and God's Remedy

The substitutionary sacrifice was both physical and spiritual. The suffering that Jesus endured was both physical and spiritual.

There are many Christians who adamantly oppose all the Bible facts that clearly state that Jesus died spiritually and went to Hell for three days.

It appears to me that these people do not spend much time reading and meditating God's Word.

In Acts 17:11 it tells us that **"These were more noble than those in Thessalonica, in that they received the Word with all readiness of**

mind, and searched the scriptures daily, whether those things were so."

It seems that some people spend their time looking through the Bible to prove something is wrong or incorrect. This scripture says that they 'searched' the Word to prove its validity.

The word 'search,' in the Greek is ANAKRINO. It means to investigate, ask questions to determine.

To do all those things takes labor and time. The Word itself tells us 'to study' (2 Timothy 2:15). If anyone wants the truth, the Holy Spirit will guide them to that truth. Are you ready to educate yourself with God's Word?

Let's start at the beginning, and that takes us to the Garden of Eden, where the first disobedience took place.

God had created man in His own image and likeness so that this new man could be in the God-class, someone with whom God could communicate. This man was perfect, he would have lived forever. He was to start God's family. What a privilege and honor. But satan steps into the garden, and convinces Eve to disobey what God had said, and Adam went along. It was a very, very serious sin. Some call it high treason, and with good reason.

Adam and Eve were told by God to create a

family for God, but they destroyed God's dream for a family that He could love and care for. They were His representatives.

As soon as they disobeyed God, they not only gave up their world dominion under God, and legally transferred it to satan, but immediately they received their new master's spiritual nature, which is death. Satan's nature was death, Spiritual Death.

Because sin is spiritual, that death that satan gave them went into their spirits. So their spirits became dead, and so we can assuredly call that spiritual death, "death in the spirit of man.

When God made Adam and Eve, God put His own nature in them, that nature was eternal life. But when they sold out to satan, God's nature and life went out of Adam and Eve, and satan's nature, spiritual death, went into them.

Spiritual death is not physical death. It is not cessation of life, because we know that God told Adam that in the very day he ate of that forbidden tree, that very day he would surely die.

Adam and Eve died that day because God said they would. They died in their spirits. Spiritual Death entered their spirits, but as we know, Adam lived physically for another 930 years.

When he died spiritually, his physical body lived on. His spirit received satan's nature which is eternal death. When Adam disobeyed God, he legally turned over the earth to satan, and satan gave Adam his death. That death went into Adam's spirit. I believe that all who read what I just said truly understand now what Spiritual Death is. Adam and Eve exchanged God's nature, which is eternal life, with the nature of satan, which is eternal death.

Now, Adam has no way to make himself right with God by himself. Eve is in the same situation and there is no way she can take herself out of this eternal death by herself.

Their situation is one of hopelessness. God had to drive them out of the garden before they could eat from the Tree of Life, because in doing so would cause them to live forever in spiritual death.

Now, there is a long Biblical history of how God began to lay out His plan to reinstate His man, and bring them out of Spiritual Death and back into His eternal life. But I shall bring us forward in that history up to Jesus' birth.

His incarnation was the key to our redemption. In John's Gospel he said, **"...the Word was made flesh, and dwelt among us, and we beheld His glory, the glory as of the only begotten of the Father, full of grace and truth."** (John 1:14)

Man needs a mediator, but he has none. I told you in this chapter earlier that man is hopeless. There is no hope at all.

Again by Adam's treason, his disobedience, he forfeited his dominion over the earth, he gave it to satan, and now satan has a legal position controlling the earth.

Man is hopeless, Godless, and now man is under all the sway of his new master. In fact, Adam has come into union with satan. What satan has, Adam had, spiritual death.

Exodus 33:20 describes this condition Adam has sold out to. He was abandoned by God, all communication ceased.

"And He said, Thou cans't not see My face: for there shall no man see Me, and live."

Before the fall of Adam he walked with God in the cool of the day. He talked with God. Where Adam had all that was beautiful and perfect, now devastation had taken its place.

Even the peaceful animal kingdom had turned to killing one another. The vegetation had begun to get thorned.

Adam's sin made him mortal, or death-doomed. Only spiritual life can make him immortal. But how will that happen?

Eternal life can only come from the life-giver through His grace and we can receive it by faith in Jesus Christ. Listen, man has not only become sin with satan's sin, but he is a transgressor and a child of the devil. He cannot come into the presence of God as he is, spiritually dead.

Man needs a new birth, a new kind of nature, a kind of nature that comes from God. Because Adam was our representative man, we got what he got. He died spiritually, so did we. We have identified with Adam's sin.

To identify means to make identical and treat as the same.

So, the exact way that God treats Adam, he has to treat us. We have identified with Adam's sin because he represented us.

As I said earlier, man can do nothing to help himself. A sinner cannot help another sinner.

I quoted also, earlier that **"the Word became flesh, and dwelt among us…"**

We come to God's great plan of Salvation for mankind. God had to find a way that He could legally identify with man. God had to find a way to bring His nature back into man.

First of all, Jesus, in becoming flesh, had to be done in such a way that it could not go through a natural generation.

If **"…all have sinned, and come short of the glory of God"** (Romans 3:23) and God would let Jesus come into this earth through a natural birth, then Jesus would receive spiritual death, from His mother. Then He could not be the

Redeemer. A sinner cannot save a sinner.

So, what did God do? Hebrews 10:5 tells us that God prepared a body for Jesus.

"Wherefore when He cometh into the world, He saith, Sacrifice and offering thou wouldest not, but a body has thou prepared me…"

There would be no worldly legal authority over this body that God made for Jesus.

Incarnation satisfied the yearning of man to be visited by deity, and unionized with deity.

This would make a man both man and God. A sinless man not touched by Adam's sin, his spiritual death.

If God is all powerful, then He can make a child and put it into the womb of a woman. We must believe what the Bible says. Now, here's where the genius of God is seen in His creation of a woman. In her reproductive organs lies the genius of God.

The woman's eggs do not contain the ability to make blood. The same is true about man's sperm or spermatozoon, it cannot by itself. But when joined with the egg, blood is formed, and its type is established at that instant. So how did God prevent tainted blood from flowing into the bloodstream of baby Jesus in Mary's womb. The placenta stops the flow of the blood of the mother from going into the bloodstream of the baby. God put the blood into Jesus as the Holy Spirit placed that tiny baby into Mary's womb as Jesus left heaven and entered into Mary.

Leviticus 17:11 says **"...the life of the flesh *is* in the blood..."**

God's life is in Jesus' blood, and it is the life or nature of God.

God and man are finally united. This was a true incarnation. This incarnation of Jesus is a true one, and this makes immortality a reality, and therefore Christianity is supernatural.

Now, Jesus is a God-man and as man, He can become our representative man, and therefore can identify with us. The whole incarnation is proof that Jesus pre-existed.

Man cannot be redeemed without an incarnation, because man is spiritually dead and has no approach to God, remember, he is hopeless without God. He cannot save himself.

This union of Deity and humanity will be the way a substitution can be set up. This incarnate one can stand as man's mediator, being equal with God, and can bridge the gap, bring the two together. This is the way God had chosen to assume the obligations of the human race in their treason and satisfy the claims of Justice.

Genesis 3:15 gives us what God said to satan

right after the fall about incarnation. I will pull out just one of God's four statements:

"And I will put enmity between thee and the woman, and between thy seed and her seed..."

What is satan's seed? Those who follow satan, those not born again. Woman's seed is what? The woman has no seed. The man has the seed, so what has God said here?

God said that a woman will have a child without the seed of a natural man. There will be a child without a natural generation. It's all of God and His love and grace. And one more important thing from these four things that God said and [He] **"shall bruise thy head..."**

That means that the authority of the ruler (satan) will be cut off. His rulership is cut off. He will have no more power. His lordship is over. Satan was given notice of what was to come.

Isaiah 7:13-14

"...Behold, a virgin shall conceive, and bear a son, and shall call His name Immanuel."

What a name! And that name means 'God with us.' This is incarnation. It's all from God, and of God. Adam was created by God, and gave him the honor and privilege of starting God's family through natural generation.

God had to prepare a body for Jesus, and God put His own blood into this little body of Jesus and placed it into Mary's womb. Jesus had divine blood, which the Father put in that tiny body.

Jesus lived a holy life, pleasing His father always doing His will.

Jesus came to be the second representative of the human race. He faced satan as Adam did, but this Son of man beat satan, and beat down all of satan's temptation.

Not only is Jesus our representative, but now He can identify with the human race, and He becomes our substitute. He is our substitutionary sacrifice. A substitute is one who takes another's place.

Let me regress for a moment and ask you a question. When you and I and the whole human race identified with Adam's sin that he got from satan, this spiritual death, again, where did this sin go? It went into our spirits. Sin is spiritual. It is not physical, it didn't lodge itself any place on our bodies.

Satan's nature was spiritual death, and that was passed on to Adam, and on to us. Look at Romans 5:12.

"Wherefore, as by one man sin entered

into the world, and death by sin; and so death passed upon all men, for all have sinned..."

Romans 5:16

"And not as it was by one that sinned, so is the gift, for the judgment was by one to condemnation, but the free gift is of many offenses unto justification."

What did that sin do to the human race? It condemned us. That means, that without someone able to stand in for us, our punishment would have damned us to Hell.

It was an eternal punishment for the whole human race. So Jesus identifies with the human race, and as our substitutionary sacrifice, Jesus is crucified. Jesus was on that cross as our sin bearer. In 2 Corinthians 5:21 it says, **"For He hath made Him to be sin for us, who knew no sin; that we might be made the righteousness of God in Him."**

God made Jesus sin with our sin. The Father laid on Jesus the sin of the world. That was Adam's sin passed on to us. It was called spiritual death, which He got from satan.

Again, sin is spiritual, so, where did God put that sin on Jesus? On His back? On His foot? No. He put that sin of Spiritual Death in Jesus' spirit.

Jesus became sin with our sin, and when that happened, the Father turned His back on Him.

43

Jesus asked with a loud voice, **"My God, My God, why hast Thou forsaken Me?"**

As with Adam, the communication with God had stopped. Jesus identified with our fallen state, He took our sin. He became mortal, death doomed.

Jesus was made to be sin. He took our sin, Spiritual Death into His spirit, and He became spiritually dead.

Jesus took all that we were so we could have all He would become after His resurrection. We had to identify with this representative man, and all that He became was ours the instant we received Him as Saviour.

I hope that this issue of Adam's sin is clear in your mind and heart now.

In our next chapter we will discuss Spiritual Death in detail.

Be not ignorant, brethren. You have the Word of God, study and meditate this Word of Life.

There are so many Christians who refuse the truth of The Bible because they let their senses dictate to them what feels_reasonable. Let go of that ignorance and search and seek for God's Revelation on any subject.

(John 16:13)

"The Holy Spirit will guide you into all truth."

CHAPTER

4

Spiritual Death

In our last chapter we spoke about spiritual death. Because Jesus was our substitute, He had to take upon himself all that we were, in order to give us all that He would become in His death, burial and resurrection.

He identified with us in our sin or death that condemned us and that condemnation had a punishment, a severe punishment attached to it. It meant eternal banishment from God's presence in Hell. Jesus paid that debt for all of us. Let's look at what happened to Jesus during His crucifixion. And through our sensual minds, we can only see His physical suffering. But much more was happening in His soul and spirit.

His physical sufferings were very important. He had to shed His blood unto death. And here is where many Christians show their ignorance about Jesus' blood being shed. It had to be unto death. And remember, His blood was divine. It was from His Father when He prepared Him a body.

But many say that once His blood was shed, then our sins have been wiped out and we are saved at that point, while Jesus is still alive. That is not true. If you tell these people Jesus had to do more for you to be saved, they can't believe it. So, let me prove my point by taking you to a very important scripture.

1 Corinthians 15:16-18

"For if the dead rise not, then is not Christ raised. And if Christ be not raised, your faith [is] vain; ye are yet in your sins. Then they also which are fallen asleep in Christ are perished."

It is obvious that Christ must be raised from the dead before your sins are forgiven. This scripture also shuts down another important statement from those who do not study the Word concerning the crucifixion. They say when Jesus said, **"It is finished,"** that meant that there is nothing more to be done.

Well, He hasn't taken our place as our substitute to pay the debt for our sin. We still have the *Adamic* nature in our spirits, and Jesus has not taken us out of Spiritual Death. Also, His own pangs of death haven't been removed. And by the way, do you know what those pangs of death are that Jesus had experienced?

Is there any pain in death? We put 'RIP' on grave stones. If there are pains while we are dead physically, why put RIP on the headstones?

Those pains that Jesus was enduring were not physical, He had died on the cross, His physical body was not feeling pain. He was physically dead.

But because Jesus, as our substitutionary sacrifice, had to identify with our sins, then God had to treat Him the same as He would us.

Remember the definition I gave you of 'to identify?' It means to make identical and treat as the same.

Do not forget that when Adam sinned, he committed high treason, the whole human race identified with him because he was our representative man. So God had to treat us just as he would treat Adam because, as Paul said in Romans 5:12, **"...death passed upon all men..."**

We entered into Adam's sin, and therefore, we were due the same punishment. A debt had to be paid. We had to go to Hell. But the good news is that Jesus took our place, He would pay our debt for us. We were spiritually dead. Death was in our spirits.

So Jesus, being a representative man, identified with us in every aspect of what Adam's consequence was, and would take the place of fallen humanity. He became our substitute. Just a reminder to my readers, I write these things out of a spirit of love. I love the Body of Christ. But often, I hear some of those members, yes, out of ignorance, say things that are not biblical. We cannot just ignore them, no more than Paul could.

Paul said, **"...I would not have you to be ignorant, brethren..."** (1 Thessalonians 4:13)

So, I am trying to pull together many of these ignorances that so many well-meaning, Christ-loving Christians express, and bring those misunderstandings into the light of the true gospel of Christ.

So, if Spiritual Death is the absence of the life of God, and is the nature of satan passed down through Adam to the whole human race, obviously we need to get out of that place called Spiritual Death.

Well, God's plan for the whole human race is in a person called Jesus Christ, the only Son of God.

The spotless Lamb of God is going to be our substitutionary sacrifice. Then He must identify with each one completely in all aspects.

While Jesus was on the cross going through physical agony, His blood was being shed, and it had to be shed unto death, as I just said. So after hanging there on Calvary's Cross, being crucified, that is, he's suffering, and in about three hours, God is going to put all our sin into Jesus' spirit.

Do not forget that sin is spiritual, so God is not going to put this sin on Jesus' body, but in His spirit.

As I mentioned in a previous chapter, in 2 Corinthians 5:21, we see this Divine exchange taking place, and this is where Jesus identifies with us totally. God puts our sin, our sin nature, the one we got from Adam, transferred from satan, into Jesus' spirit.

This nature is Spiritual Death, that is, satan's nature is death, and it was in our spirit. 2 Corinthians 5:21 clearly shows us what God did to Jesus.

"For He hath made him to *be* sin for us, who knew no sin; that we might be made the righteousness of God in Him."

God took our sin nature, Spiritual Death, and made Jesus sin with our sin. Our sin made Jesus spiritually dead, Death in Jesus' Spirit.

Notice that sin, is singular, not sins. It was the nature of satan that bound us, and caused us to commit sins. As soon as God made Jesus sin with our sin in His spirit, He died spiritually. His spirit received the nature of satan. He identified with us. He had to become what we were, so we could receive God's righteousness through Jesus. (2 Corinthians 5:21)

When that happened, Jesus was still alive physically. He was still breathing, and then said these remarkable words, **"My God, my God, why hast Thou forsaken Me?"**

God turned His back on Jesus because He was now our sin-bearer. He was made sin with our sin.

The scripture says in Ezekiel 18:20, **"The soul that sinneth, it shall die."**

Once Jesus becomes sin with our sin, He is spiritually dead, and now He can die physically because He is now mortal, meaning death- doomed.

Turn to Isaiah 53:9

"And He made His grave with the wicked, and with the rich in His death; because He had done no violence, neither was any deceit in His mouth."

If you look at the foot notes and scriptural references at the bottom of this page, in Isaiah 53:9, the word *'death'* in this context is plural, *'deaths.'*

Jesus died spiritually when the Father made

Jesus sin with our sin, again, He became mortal, and then gave up the Ghost, His spirit left His body. As we all know from the Word of God, when we die physically, our spirits leave our bodies, and go immediately to judgment.

Hebrews 9:27 says **"And as it is appointed unto men once to die, but after this the judgment..."**

So Jesus' judgment was our judgment, He took our sin and now He is taking our place in carrying out our penalty. He took our debt, that is, we were to go to Hell, and He suffered in our place, and paid our debt for us, and Hell is where He paid our penalty.

There are some ignorant Christians who object to Jesus going to Hell. "Not my sweet Jesus," they say. "My Lord never went to Hell." Some even call us heretics for saying such things.

So, once again, what do the scriptures say? Please pay attention to what these scriptures say, and accept the truth of what they say, and "be not ignorant, brethren."

Let us look at what Peter said in Acts 2:23-31.

"Him, be delivered by the determinate counsel and foreknowledge of God, ye have taken, and by wicked hands have crucified and slain: Whom God hath raised

up, having loosed the pains of death: because it was not possible that He should be holden of it. For David speaketh concerning Him, I foresaw the Lord always before my face, for He is on my right hand, that I should not be moved: Therefore did my heart rejoice, and my tongue was glad; moreover also my soul shall rest in hope: Because Thou wilt not leave my soul in Hell, neither wilt Thou suffer thine Holy One to see corruption. Thou hast made known to me the ways of life; Thou shalt make me full of joy with Thy countenance. Men [and] brethren, let me freely speak unto you of the patriarch David, that he is both dead and buried, and his sepulcher is with us unto this day. Therefore being a prophet, and knowing that God had sworn with an oath to him, that of the fruit of his loins, according to the flesh, he would raise up Christ to sit on his throne; He seeing this before spake of the resurrection of Christ, that his soul was not left in Hell, neither his flesh did see corruption."

Acts 16:10 is where Peter references Acts 2:31. **"He seeing this before spake of the resurrection of Christ, that His soul was not left in Hell, neither His flesh did see corruption."**

Acts 13:35 speaks of Jesus' resurrection, when it is spoken about **"thou shalt not suffer**

Thine Holy One to see corruption."

The word *'soul'* in Acts 2 is PSUCHE, meaning spirit. If it means literally soul, as some contend, the soul cannot be separated from the spirit of man. So, what happened to the spirit of Jesus in Hell? He was suffering for us, everything that was due us. For three days, as Isaiah said in the great redemptive chapter, Isaiah 53, **He was wounded for our transgressions. He was bruised for our iniquities.** (Isaiah 53:5)

And in Isaiah 53:4 — the Prophet speaks in strong, precise words of what God did to Jesus.

"Surely He hath borne our griefs, (Hebrew word CHOLI, meaning disease, sickness and malady) **and carried our sorrows:** (Hebrew word MAKOB meaning pain, anguish and affliction) **yet we did esteem Him stricken, smitten of God, and afflicted."**

All these things were happening in Hell to Jesus' spirit. It had to be so because sin is spiritual, and the suffering in Hell is because of sin. Sin was in our spirits and Jesus took them into His spirit, and that's where He was wounded and bruised, and by His stripes we were healed.

There are those who do not believe that healing is in the redemptive work of Jesus. They deny it even after reading Isaiah 53. But they neglect to look at Matthew 8:16 and 17.

It says there very clearly:

"When the even was come, they brought unto Him many that were possessed with devils: and He cast out the spirits with *His* Word, and healed all that were sick: That it might be fulfilled which was spoken by Esaias the prophet, saying, Himself took our infirmities, and bare our sicknesses."

This is referring to Isaiah 53:4. Now look at what 1 Peter 2:24 says: **"Who His own self bare our sins in His own body on the tree, that we being dead to sins, should live unto righteousness; by Whose stripes ye were healed."**

We need to take God at His Word. As long as we remain in Sense-Knowledge, we will never get Revelation-Knowledge from God. Many Christians like to think of their relationship with the Lord as some kind of a feely-touchy, warm and fuzzy, feel-good kind of religion. That all belongs to the Sense-Knowledge realm. The true Believer has a relationship with the Father and Jesus, through the Word with the Holy Spirit's guidance. Seek revealed knowledge by meditating God's Word, yes, day and night.

CHAPTER

5

Ignorance...Be Gone!

I will pick out some verses to show you what Paul, the Apostle, told Timothy, wanting him to cultivate and develop what he, Paul, and other witnesses have taught about Jesus and the Word of God.

2 Timothy 1:13-14

"Hold fast the form of sound words, which thou hast heard of me, in faith and love which is in Christ Jesus. That good thing that was committed unto thee, keep by the Holy Ghost which dwelleth in us."

Then in 2 Timothy 2:15 Paul encourages Timothy to **"Study to shew thyself approved unto God, a workman that needed not to be ashamed, rightly dividing the Word of truth."**

Look at the Word '*study*,' the Greek word is SPONDAZO, it means to endeavor with a labor of a diligent nature expecting excellent results.

But notice that this study is not, first of all, primarily for your personal education. It is seeking God's approval that we are looking for first. His approval will only come when He sees that we have been diligently laboring to dig out the absolute truth of His Word, so we can know it and live it.

In 2 Timothy 1:13 we have been told to hold fast to sound words. Also in Hebrews 4:14 and Hebrews 10:23 we see these words repeated, '*hold fast.*'

In Hebrews 4:14 it tells us to hold fast to our profession. In Hebrews 10:23, again, it tells us to hold fast to our profession of our faith without wavering. The reason given for this is because He that promised is faithful. We can put our faith and confidence in His Word and in Him.

I will come back to this word *profession* in a moment, but there is something that goes hand in hand with your study of the Word.

We see this in Joshua 1:8, where it says that, **"This Book of the Law shall not depart out of thy mouth; but thou shalt meditate therein day and night, that thou mayest observe to do**

according to all that is written therein: for then thou shalt make thy way prosperous, and then thou shalt have good success."

The Word meditate is the Hebrew word HAGAH, which means *"to ponder with pleasure and murmur."* It is likened to a cow chewing his cud. He chews and chews, trying to get the most out of it.

In 1Timothy we see further instruction from Paul, in:

1 Timothy 4:12

"Let no man despise thy youth; but be thou an example of the Believers, in Word, in conversation, in charity, in spirit, in faith, in purity." And verse 15 goes on to say, **"Meditate upon these things; give thyself wholly to them; that thy profiting may appear to all."**

So we see that with our studying, we must meditate God's Word, and invite the Holy Spirit to lead us to all truth. He will guide us to the truth. All this takes labor on our part. We diligently give ourselves to be approved by God. His approval will come when he sees that we are spending time in His Word, studying, meditating and holding fast to what God reveals to us, then we act upon it, that's what Paul told Timothy, observe it to do it.

It takes intimate time in the presence of the Holy Spirit who will guide you to all truth.

Now let me get back to that word *'profession'* that Paul used twice in writing to Timothy. Let's look where it comes from.

Go to 2 Corinthians 4:13, it says:

"We having the same spirit of faith, according as it is written, I believed, and therefore have I spoken; we also believe, and therefore speak…"

If you want the same Spirit of Faith, then your speech must be according to how it is written. You cannot put your own interpretation on what is written. It says, **"…according as it is written, I believed, and therefore have I spoken…"** in other words, I repeat exactly what God says.

In the Greek language it is called HOMOLOGEO, it means to say the same as. The meaning conveys the idea of a profession, which in Greek is confession. You profess, or confess what God says. This saying what God says comes from the Word HOMOU, which means united together in the same place. HOMOU and HOMOLOGEO basically are the same. They mean that we are in agreement and united as one with God's Words. It is a confession. It is an outward profession of what we believe in our hearts.

A good example of this is in the form of one of God's principles.

Look at Romans 10:3-10

"For they being ignorant of God's righteousness, and going about to establish their own righteousness, have not submitted themselves unto the righteousness of God."

(Did you notice in this verse that these people were ignorant because they had their own idea of how to obtain righteousness, and did not do what God's Word said about it; but Paul will show them how.)

"For Christ *is* the end of the law for righteousness to everyone that believeth."

(The law was their school master, but they didn't listen to what was being taught, that is, they couldn't keep the law, but continued to sin in it.) The law was to show them how sinful sin was, and that they couldn't keep from sinning. Then in verse 6, we learn how to obtain righteousness which is of faith — and faith speaks this way,

"...Say not in thine heart, Who shall ascend into heaven? (that is, to bring Christ down

61

from above)... **Or, Who shall descend into the deep? (That is, to bring up Christ again from the dead). But what saith it? The word is nigh thee,** *even* **in thy mouth, and in thy heart; that is, the word of faith, which we preach; That if thou shalt confess with thy mouth the Lord Jesus, and shalt believe in thine heart that God hath raised Him from the dead, thou shalt be saved. For with the heart man believeth unto righteousness; and with the mouth confession is made unto salvation."**

The Word *'salvation'* is the Greek word SOTERIA, and it has manifold meanings, but all confirm what God desires for us all; eternal life, preservation, protection, health, healing, and prosperity. Can you see God's loving-kindness in these words? So God has told us a principle to obtain the full salvation that Jesus paid for.

All is ours if we believe what God says, and make a profession or confession of faith according to what God said.

We cannot say something that God did not say. We have to say the same as God says. It becomes our confession of our faith, and we hold fast to our confession. Once we make our confession of God's Word, saying what He says, then we act on it in faith.

Hebrews 3:1

"Wherefore, holy brethren, partakers of the heavenly calling, consider the Apostle and High Priest of our profession, Christ Jesus..."

The Word *'profession'* is the Greek word HOMOLOGIA, which means the same as confession, HOMOLOGEO. Both mean *'to say the same as,' 'to agree with.'* We agree with God's Word. So we say what He says.

If He says we are the righteousness of God in Christ Jesus, we say the same thing. It doesn't matter whether we feel righteous or not. God says we are.

If God says we are holy brethren, it matters not if we don't feel holy. We still are because God says we are.

If God says that by His Son's stripes we are healed, it doesn't matter what or how we feel. We say what God says. We are healed by the stripes of Jesus. The reason there is so much argument about saying we are healed by His Son's stripes is because the opponents say that healing is not in the atonement. Are they right? No.

Let's just let the scriptures prove that healing is in the atonement and belongs to all Believers. Let's start with:

Romans 5:12

"Wherefore, as by one man sin entered into the world, and death by sin..."

Sin brought death. And sickness and disease are incipient death. So if sin brought death, and Jesus' redemptive work removed sin, that same redemptive work removed sickness at the same time.

Let's come out of all ignorance concerning how to understand what God's Word says, so we can agree with what He says about what concerns us all, our health. Let's look at Isaiah 53:3-5. Before I quote this scripture, let me pull a couple of words out of these verses. I am going to do this because some do not believe what these words say. They ascribe to these words, meanings that are not true. What did God say, and will He back it up with other scriptures?

Verse 3 has two words that are repeated. The first word is *'sorrows.'* In Hebrew, this word is MAKOB. It means pain, affliction, hurt. The second word is *'grief'*. In Hebrew it is the word CHOLI, and means sickness, disease and malady. No other meaning can honestly be given to these words, and through the Holy Spirit, He inter-weaves words that refer to both physical and spiritual suffering, as Jesus endured both this in Isaiah 53:3-5 and is about atonement. It is speaking about the expiator, Jesus Christ the Son of God, our substitutionary sacrifice. He took our place. He is called our Redeemer. To redeem means to recover ownership by paying a sum. Jesus paid so we could be totally restored to our former state, which was sinless and physically whole.

Isaiah 53:3-5

"He is despised and rejected of men; a man of sorrows, and acquainted with grief: and we hid as it were [our] faces from Him; He was despised, and we esteemed Him not. Surely He hath borne our griefs, and carried our sorrows: yet we did esteem Him stricken, smitten of God, and afflicted. But He [was] wounded for our transgressions, [He was] bruised for our iniquities: the chastisement of our peace [was] upon Him; and with His stripes we are healed."

Now watch the Holy Spirit confirm the healing that Jesus gave us in Matthew 8:16-17, referring to Isaiah 53. I showed you this in an earlier chapter, but read it again.

"When the even was come, they brought unto Him many that were possessed with devils; and He cast out the spirits with {His} Word, and healed all that were sick..."

Now listen to the Holy Spirit tell you that

Isaiah spoke of actual sickness (CHOLI) in Isaiah 53:5.

Matthew 8:17

"That it might be fulfilled which was spoken by Esaias the prophet, saying Himself took our infirmities, and bare {our} sicknesses."

To deny this meaning actual sickness and disease was not the thing that Jesus bore for us, is saying that the Holy Spirit contradicted Himself in Matthew 8:16-17, or Isaiah 53:4-5 is not true.

Further, I'll give you more scripture you can agree with, so you won't be ignorant any longer. Let God be True and all men liars.

Luke 4:18

"The Spirit of the Lord *is* **upon Me, because He hath anointed Me** (Jesus is speaking) **to preach the gospel to the poor. He hath sent Me to heal the broken hearted, to preach deliverance to the captives, and recovering of sight to the blind,** (that is healing) **to set at liberty them that are bruised, To preach the acceptable year of the Lord."** (That means the 50th year, or the Year of Jubilee.)

Jesus Himself taught us in Luke 4:19 that He was anointed to preach the acceptable year of the Lord. What this means is that the Year of

Jubilee, to which He referred in this passage, that He was to preach the gospel, and then He lists all these blessings, and Jesus hooks together the Year of Jubilee and the gospel.

When we look in the book of Leviticus 25:9, it appears that the blessings of the Year of Jubilee could not be proclaimed until the trumpet sounded, until the Day of Atonement.

On this day of the Atonement a bull was slain as a sin offering, that the Mercy Seat be sprinkled with blood. Until that moment, no mercy could be granted because the seat would be a seat of Judgment.

What this tells us is that no blessings of the gospel era could be offered until the atonement took place.

In Luke 4:18, it shows us that Jesus' ministry of healing began on the day He spoke this scripture. As you read on, you will see how the Father views this.

Luke 4:20

"And He closed the book, and He gave it again to the minister, and sat down. And the eyes of all them that were in the synagogue were fastened on Him. And He began to say unto them, This day is this scripture fulfilled in your ears."

Acts 10:38

"How God anointed Jesus of Nazareth with the Holy Ghost and with power: Who went about doing good, and healing all that were oppressed of the devil; for God was with Him."

Listen, when Adam fell in the garden, he represented all of us in the human race. So we all lost everything in the fall. But Jesus recovered it all through His redemption. I just mentioned the Year of Jubilee. Let's put this in order again.

First the atonement, the sacrifice of a bull, then the sounding of the trumpet of the Jubilee, with this declaration, **"...and ye shall return every man to his possession..."**

What a redemption, a time of liberty. Jesus came to proclaim that liberty by healing the sick.

In Numbers 21:9 all the Israelites were healed by looking at the brazen serpent which was lifted up as a type of atonement.

In Job 33:24, 25 we can read, **"...I have found a ransom,** (atonement) **his flesh shall be fresher than a child's, he shall return to the days of his youth."** (Job's flesh was healed through the atonement.)

Psalms 103:1-5

"...Who forgiveth all thine iniquities; who

healeth all thy diseases... thy youth is renewed like the eagle's."

Let me just for a moment answer the opposition on their believing that healing is not in the atonement. When looking at Matthew 8:17 there is this objection that this doesn't refer to any atonement because when Isaiah spoke this, Christ was not yet crucified, so He was not fulfilling that. So Jesus did not bear our sicknesses on the cross, but when he walked the land of Israel, He was living an atoning life.

Well, let's answer this. Did Jesus forgive our iniquities while walking the land of Israel?

Listen to me, isn't Jesus *'the Lamb of God slain from the foundation of the world?'* (Revelation 13:8) (The Father saw the whole redemptive act as already complete from the foundation of the world)

Jesus, of course, healed disease and sickness before Calvary, and if you remember, He also forgave sins.

Both forgiveness of sins and healing were done by Jesus on the grounds of the redemption of what was to come in the future.

It is time to give up your denominational false defense about healing and start saying what God's Word says. But if you want to stay in your Biblical ignorance, then keep your sickness, your pain. But if you say that God is the One who gave your disease, or sickness, or pain — for His glory , or to teach you something, then don't dare to go to the doctor or take medicine to get rid of what is bothering you, or you would be going against God's will.

Just grin and bear it until He takes it off. Ignorance, be gone!

Start agreeing what God's word really says, keep saying it and don't dig up that seed of God's Word, or you'll never get a harvest. Say, **"By His stripes I am healed."**

Put that seed of health in your heart with your tongue, but don't dig it up the next day by contradicting what God said. Keep watering that seed, pull up the weeds, and your health will soon bloom.

Follow Proverbs 4:20-21

1 **Attend to my word**
2 **Incline thine ear unto my sayings**
3 **Do not let them depart from thine eyes**
4 **Keep them in the middle of your heart**

They are life and health to your flesh.

Do you read what you believe? Or do you believe what you read? Open your heart to the Holy Spirit, and He will guide you to all truth.

It doesn't say He will lead you to all truth. He will guide you. It's up to you to dig in and study, meditate and plant God's Word in your heart.

Before you realize it, your ignorance of God's Word will be gone!

Richard Mallette, was born in Athol, Massachusetts in a Catholic family. He studied for four years for the priesthood in Seminary.

However, this was not God's call on his life. Twenty- five years later, Richard and his wife Adrienne learned of Christ and received Him as Lord and Savior. Shortly thereafter they were baptized in the Holy Spirit.

Under the direction of his pastor and church, Richard began a ministry in his home. That ministry grew at a phenomenal rate growth to two thousand members by the year 2000. The ministry was called Living Word Ministries, and during those years, two church buildings were built, one in 1989 and the other in 2000. The flock was well established in the Word of God.

Pastor Mallette retired from pastoral ministry. He traveled for five years in New England and in New York State teaching at seminars and in churches. He has since been led to establish another church which is presently called "New Heart Christian Church," with fifty members and growing. His emphasis is the same on "Who you are in Christ" and understanding the reason for the Cross.

www.ingramcontent.com/pod-product-compliance
Lightning Source LLC
Chambersburg PA
CBHW060038050426
42448CB00012B/3064